THE DOG OWNER'S BOOK OF POOP AND PEE!

MIKE DEATHE

CPDT-KA

PUBLISHED BY FASTPENCIL

Second Edition

Copyright ©

Sale of this book without a front cover may be unauthorized. If the book is coverless, it may have been reported to the publisher as "unsold or destroyed" and neither the author nor the publisher may have received payment for it.

http://www.fastpencil.com

Printed in the United States of America

Table of Contents

What is Potty Training ?	13
The Crate . . . Use It!	17
Mistakes Equal Bad Habits	23
Choosing "The Potty Spot"	27
How To Know They Gotta Go...	31
The Doggy Doorbell	35
Is Punishment a Bad Thing?	39
What To Do If We Find Puddles and Piles	43
One More Possibility	47
Conclusion	49
Afterword	51

This book is written for those who have pulled their hair out wondering why Fido won't just "GO" where he is supposed to. I hope you can, with the help of this book, better learn to speak DASL (Dog As a Second Language) and get your potty puzzle under control!

First, I want to thank Kate for her unending help in writing, editing and putting up with me through the process of writing this book, and Sarah for her help in editing the second edition. Also, thanks go out to Dr. Ian Dunbar who has, through his work with dogs, helped me find my own voice. I know I will forget someone, but let me extend thanks to Kim for making me realize I could train dogs; to Jenn for giving me the chance to teach someone else how to train dogs; to Pat for believing in me and helping me achieve my goal of my own training center; and finally to all those others, dog and human, who have helped me grow, learn and follow the idea of KEEPING IT SIMPLE STUPID! Thank you, Mike

In 2008, while working as a dog trainer, I started a business, **Muttz "R" Us.com.** This was an on-line t-shirt and unique dog-training product company with a simple motto: Adopt a Pet & Save a Life! The basic idea was to sell funny T-Shirts that poked fun at purebred dogs in order to draw attention to the importance of adopting and not buying dogs. I had seen over time just how many dogs (and cats) were being euthanized each and every year for no other reason than they could not find a home.

Soon after that, I started volunteering for the Humane Society of Greater Kansas City and it became apparent that just finding homes for these animals was not enough! Why was it that people were surrendering and giving up on their beloved family pets? The answer quickly became obvious: problem behaviors!

I had been writing articles for a local pet magazine, as well as for my own pet blog, when the idea came to me. Why not write concise, affordable books and eBooks for everyday pet owners, to address all the reasons I had heard for giving up on their furry, four-legged best friends? I did not want to write a book of instruction, because as we all know, very few of us ever consistently follow them. But what if I wrote a book about understanding the difference in the ways humans and dogs relate to each other? And with that knowledge, plus a few helpful tips, we'd have you and Fido actually working together, not against one another . . .

The Keep it Simple Stupid **Dog Owner's Book of Poop and Pee** is just that: an easy to read, and an even easier to understand guide to getting Fido to "go" at the right time, in the right place, without ruining your carpet and without pulling your hair out in the process. Don't get me wrong, this is not one of those "potty train your dog in three easy steps" books. I know (and deep down, so do you) that this is a process over time, not a quick fix.

There is no magic spell, silver bullet or Jedi mind trick to make it happen any faster. Rather, I hope to teach you the right way to solve this bathroom riddle, using common sense and humor. I'll cover some tried-and-true ways to "speak dog" in the hopes of making this process easier. In the end, my goal is to save a few dogs from being deposited on the front steps of the local shelter. If I can do that with you, then I've done my job! I hope you enjoy this book. It was fun to write – and to a guy who never thought he could string together two coherent thoughts, this is a real accomplishment!

- Mike

P.S. As far as that "two coherent thoughts" line? If it wasn't for the unbelievable editing of both Kate and Sarah . . . let's just say you and I owe both of them a thank you.

What is Potty Training ?

So what is potty training? Well, I suppose it depends on your perspective. For you, the reader, it probably means *I want my dog to quit peeing and pooping all over the house.* Many dog trainers believe it comes down to *what you are going to tolerate.*

I guess if you want my view, it is simply getting Fido to understand there is no difference between his home and yours. Now, before you start worrying about whether you wasted money on this book, take a deep breath and remember: dogs are very clean animals, unless we teach them otherwise. They do not like to live in filth, or near filth. So why would your dear, loving, adorable pet leave these little surprises all over your home? One of two reasons: because you have either inadvertently taught him to, or it could be because you have never taken the time to show him exactly where the toilet is!

Think about it this way. If you have house guests and they ask where the bathroom is, what do you do? Exactly. You tell them it's down the hall, first door on the right. You might even warn them if it's dirty (you know, those darn kids!) or maybe instruct them to jiggle the handle to make sure the flapper seals! In comparison, let's look at a common method for teaching dogs:

1. Here is the door.
2. Toss dog outside said door.
3. Shut door because it's cold.
4. Lose track of time and watch TV for 10 minutes.
5. Oh crap, forgot the dog! Rush to let Fido in.
6. Fido has an accident within a few minutes.
7. Cuss out the dog.
8. Beat dog with newspaper.
9. Rub dog's nose in mess.
10. Finally, have a "serious talk" with Fido about his lack of manners, where you want him to go and how disappointed you are in him!

Oh yeah, and you probably repeat this process at least 4 or 5 times a day! Does any of this sound familiar? Now keep in mind, dogs are animals. They have no concept of the English language, or for that matter, why it is wrong to pee on this comfy, absorbent and soft stuff you keep calling carpet.

Simply put, "potty training" is nothing more than teaching Fido that your entire house is also his or her home, and the same rules apply for both. In the wild, dogs are den animals! They actually like small, secure locations where they can curl up and feel safe! In addition to this aspect of their makeup, dogs are naturally "tidy" animals, and they do not want to be in or near their own filth. If observed in the wild, dogs will move away from their den to relieve themselves. In their mind, not to do this would just be gross! The potty problem inside the house arises when the dog gets confused about where their "home" (or den) space begins, and just exactly where it ends.

Have you ever heard the old question, "What does a bear do in the woods?" The answer is the same for a dog or a bear, they pee and poop on or near the closest tree they can find! However, they do not do it in their own living room! Are we, as humans, really silly enough to think that a dog will "hold it" until they get to the next gas station or public restroom? This is just one example of how humans don't think like dogs and, thus, are faced with the inevitable potty training problems.

Aren't we the ones who brought Fido into the house in the first place? Therefore, it's our job to help them live in our world. Think of it as learning a second language.

The easiest way to start this process is to crate train. We know that dogs are den animals and they don't want to soil in or near their den, so let's use this to our advantage. When you start with crate training, you use their clean nature to teach them to "hold it" until you, the human, not only let them out but show them their special "potty spot."

Let me be clear here: if you are dealing with a puppy and just stick him in a crate, he will only hold it only as long as he physically can. Just throwing your puppy in a crate teaches the dog it's okay to poop and pee in that crate. *Mom and Dad aren't letting me out,* the puppy thinks, *and they're not showing me where the heck the bathroom is.*

At this point, ask yourself, what choice have you given the poor dog? Simply throwing the dog in the crate without the right training can lead to another bad habit: your dog just might learn to dislike the crate! That's not the goal.

A good rule of thumb when crate training puppies is that every month old the puppy is will equal one hour of bladder holding time. So, for example, an eight week old puppy (two months) should be able to hold it for approximately two hours. This is the *outside limit* of your pup's bladder and bowels, and pushing past this limit will only result in more accidents, and ultimately a longer, more frustrating experience in house training! Hey, no one said this was going to be easy! If you are already thinking that this sounds like a lot of work, you may want to consider a goldfish rather than a dog... but I digress.

To start the training process right, during the first week the puppy comes home, you must take Fido to the specific "potty spot" every hour on the hour during the day, and use the above rule of thumb (on frequency of visits to the potty spot) at night while they are in the crate! Yes, you will have to set your alarm, put on your robe, and actually take the dog outside in the middle of the night; You might even have to do it more than once per night starting off!

If you leave your puppy in the crate any longer than the time they can hold it, expect accidents, plus the possible side effect of teaching Fido it is okay to soil the crate. If you thought potty training was already hard, imagine trying to teach a dog who is already okay with soiling where he lives! So, now you have to get busy teaching your dog more than just potty training. Your dog must learn not only to prevent accidents, but also to begin teaching good potty habits, including when and where!

I am a big believer that a bad habit never learned is a good habit created. So consider the idea of "Mistake-Free" potty training. When I talk of fanatical training, I simply mean good management. If I actually pay attention to a dog for the first 60 days and make sure Fido only relieve himself in one spot (the one I choose) and never let him make a mistake (the paying attention part), then what will the dog learn? Potty training! Isn't that the problem you are having and the reason you bought this book? All mistakes can be fixed and all frustrations can become wins. So turn the page and let's get to fixing!

The Crate ... Use It!

Some among us feel crate training is cruel. Here, again, is another example of pushing human ideas onto our canine friends. What you like, dislike, or even think about living in a crate has absolutely nothing to do with what Fido thinks about it. Whether the crate training process has gone well or not, the goal is to look at life as your dog would. Avoid forcing your human idea of life on the dog. Let's get past opinions of crates, and look at some common crate training mistakes.

The first night at home with the puppy, the owner puts the dog in the crate. And guess what? The dog cried. The owner, feeling like the dog hates the crate, lets the dog out.

So what has this owner taught their dog? *If I cry, these new people come and get me!* Anyone who has had small kids is probably reminiscing on past adventures in child rearing, and bedtime. When the dog was crying, it had nothing to do with the crate. Dogs are social animals, and the crying is natural. The dog just wants to be closer to their pack. To make matters worse, many people put the crate in an area as far away from the family as possible (for their own convenience) and still wonder why the dog cries.

So the new puppy is closest to the new family, the crate should be placed in the den, family room or at least a bedroom. When you let Fido out of the crate when he whines, you inadvertently enforce the idea that the crate is a bad, lonely place. If Fido simply cries, he gets what he wants: closer to the family and more attention from the people in the house! Ironic, isn't it?

Focus on making the crate a positive environment instead of solitary confinement. This eliminates the crying and anxiety. You then have a dog well on his way to liking a crate, not to mention the added benefit of a dog that, when let out, will have a full bladder and bowels, ready to make the potty pit-stop when and where you want it.

Let's not teach the wrong habits. How do we start the crate training process the right way? First, start with how to get the dog in the crate. Have the dog enter the crate on his or her own; you *do not* put the dog in the crate. Lure with treats, feed the dog in the crate, put Fido's toys in the crate and then reward him when he goes in to get them – all are fair game. What you *cannot* do is force the dog into the crate, or do anything else that negatively affects Fido's view of being in the crate.

Okay, no force allowed. Let me give you a tried-and-true trick on how to get a dog to want to go in his/her crate! Take a treat-filled dog toy (Kong is a common brand; your pet store will have several choices) and fill it with something really good, like dog food or peanut butter! Show the dog the Kong and, get Fido really interested in it. Now for the trick: toss it in the cage and shut the door before the dog can go in after it!

Now, just wait. In a matter of seconds, you will have a dog giving you the "hairy eyeball!" Fido is thinking, "Now wait just a darn minute! I want my Kong! How dare this insolent human not let me in to get it!" Let the moment build for 20-30 seconds and simply ask your pup "Would you like to go to bed?" and open the door. I will bet you anything that Fido will be quite ready to get in that crate and get that treat.

The real life issue here, bigger than treats, is that we, as owners, are lousy problem solvers. When it comes to pets, we want everything to be easy! We tend to try for the quick fix – and then we end up being the reason why our dogs dislike their crates. But just spending the necessary time and effort early on makes the associations positive. Crate training, unwanted behaviors (and even my line of work!) would disappear.

Extrapolate this idea to training in general. You can easily make the assumption that most problem behaviors, including potty training, are generally due to our actions. That's right, our actions towards dogs and our reactions to them. Makes you think!

Focus on making Fido's time in the crate as positive as possible. What does this mean to you? First, don't expect your dog to spend four hours in the crate the very first day in the new environment (that's your house!). This time must be built up, day-by-day and moment-by-moment.

People who successfully get a dog crate-trained spend weeks, not days, teaching the dog about the new space! They feed the dog in the crate, use Kongs and other interactive toys to allow the dog to get used to the crate and *slowly* build up the time spent in the cage until Fido doesn't mind his crate. Instead, he quite rather likes to nap, spend time with a chew toy or just get away from the hustle and bustle of a busy home in his crate! In a matter of speaking, it becomes his little house within your home!

The next step is to combine the act of going in the crate with a verbal cue, like "go to bed." It's a really good idea to keep a treat jar on or near the crate to reward Fido when he goes into his crate when you use the cue "go to bed."

So when should you reward Fido? Treats should not be an every time reward. Rather, treats should be given at random times. You don't want to create treat junkies; you want to create an association so positive with the crate, that the crate itself becomes a reward. Treats are to teach behaviors and reinforce them, not as a bribe or a pay-off! (I could write an entire book on this mistake, and I just might.) Suffice it to say, within 6-12 repetitions the treats don't come every time, but are given randomly to keep up interest and motivation.

In no time at all, you will have a dog happily enjoying that personal condo on cue! Go slowly, and build a positie relationship between Fido and the crate. Hurrying this association is one of the biggest mistakes many folks make. This gives the crate a negative association, and also has owners up at 3 am listening to a whining dog or even worse, cleaning up a mess!

So what do you do when the mistakes have already been made, and Fido already hates the crate? There are many ways to recondition a dog into liking the crate – except in two specific situations! Let's start with the exceptions:

- The dog is from a puppy mill
- The dog has severe separation anxiety

A dog or puppy raised in a puppy mill, having spent its entire life in a cage, has most likely learned to dislike the crate! Additionally, these dogs have also learned the only place available to relieve themselves is – guess where? – in the crate. Separation anxiety, on the other hand is about feeling trapped, but for this example, let's say you are dealing with a dog who, when crated, will damage its surroundings or injure itself. What I am talking about here is way past whining. It is not uncommon to find torn nails or broken teeth in dogs diagnosed with separation anxiety, as well as destroying crates, blinds being ripped down and all sorts of other chewed-up items.

In both of these cases, professional help will be required! If you own a dog in one of these categories, please keep reading this book so that you will have a better understanding of how potty training works. But keep in mind, a professional, positive-based dog trainer, veterinarian or behaviorist will be essential to help get you and Fido through these issues. Especially in these scenarios, asking for help is a sign of intelligence, not weakness!

What if, on the other hand, you have a dog who simply has not yet learned to like the crate? Let's look at one of the common pitfalls that can end crate training on the first night. What do you do on that first night, when you get the puppy to go into the crate and ready to go to bed . . . and then whining and crying begins? In most cases, the reaction is, "I have a job," "I need my beauty sleep," or any other excuse to convince yourself that the dog must be let out and you must be allowed to go back to sleep. *Wrong!* This should not happen!

The first several weeks of having a new dog in the house is rough. It's like when you bring a new baby into your home. If you don't do it right, you've successfully taught Fido that his human — yes, that's you — will do whatever Fido wants! You may not know it, but you will be the talk around the fire hydrant, with your dog telling all the other neighborhood hounds how easy you were to train!

Let me explain this concept with a story. Eleven years ago, I was blessed to receive a beautiful, healthy, baby boy named Donovan! I remember the time shortly after the glorious moment when I took a moment to go grab a bite to eat with my mom and dad. My mom gave me some advice, advice that ensured I not only got plenty of sleep (as a first timer in the parenting ranks), but also gave me the perfect way to teach and describe crate training in dogs. Yeah, my mom is just that smart!

She told me I needed to be ready, the first night at home with baby Donovan, for the first of many challenges with this little ball of joy. She went on to tell me that before you can put a baby to bed, all the basics must be covered. Some seemed obvious, but I, a smart son who never argues with Mom, listened. Clean diaper, full belly, crib set up and warmed up so it's comfortable, lights already dimmed . . . and the mobile turned on. All this pre-work must be completed before Donovan is ever put down in the crib, according to Mom. If you don't start bedtime off on the right foot, well then how on earth are you going to expect to get any sleep?

Even with all that work up front, Mom was fast to point out that the first week would be rough. "Donovan will test you," she said, and boy-oh-boy did he! But my mom's conversation left us forewarned and ready. She told us to expect crying for at least the first week.

But she also suggested caution. There are two types of crying, Mom said. The first happens soon after putting the baby to bed (*Hey, where did everyone go?*) and the second cry tells us something is not right (dirty diapers, hunger or pain). The next thing she said connected to dogs and crate training: if you get up and give in to Donovan right after you put him to bed, assuming you have done all the pre-work getting ready, then don't call me to ask why he is crying every time you put him to bed!

Simply put, if he goes to sleep and then wakes up several hours later crying, I had better get out of bed and go check on her grandson because he needs something. In the end, we simply had to wait him out, so rules were learned fairly but early.

I hope you are nodding your head, thinking this makes sense. But if not, let's break it down into three separate time frames:

A. Pre Work (before the dog goes to bed)
1. Give Fido both food and water, but not too close to bedtime.
2. Make sure the dog has gone outside to empty both bladder and bowels.

3. Put the dog's crate in the room where you spend the most time (living room or bedroom).

4. Put the dog to bed when lifestyle action is winding down (don't try to put the dog to bed when everyone is busy in the living room).

5. Dim the lights (or turn them off) before the dog goes to bed.

6. Prep the crate:

- A Kong with a small amount of peanut butter! Enough to keep him busy, but not so much as to fill the bowels!
- Consider a tick-tock clock near or on top of the crate (the sound is soothing especially for puppies or dogs new to your home)
- If the pup is very young, offer a Mason jar full of warm water wrapped in a towel (once again, soothing).
- If it's the first night, here's a tip: get a blanket from the breeder or shelter that has been in the dog's space. The smell of litter mates or familiarity is also soothing.
- Make sure the dog gets a treat for going in the crate on command (after he goes in, not before.) This is a reward, not a bribe!

B. Immediately after going to bed: (What do you do if the dog cries early on or right off the bat?)

1. This one is the easiest to teach but the hardest to do! Never let a dog out of the crate when the dog is crying. Doing so only teaches the dog that crying works, reinforcing the behavior and making it very hard to stop.

2. Ignore the whining or barking! If you need to, sleep on the couch. Moving the dog only draws attention to the bad behavior. Furthermore, you already decided where the dog was going to sleep, so why on earth would you change the dog's accommodations?

3. If you are about to melt down, then you **must** wait at least five seconds of silence before letting the dog out! Do not bring the dog to bed with you. Instead, take Fido to the "potty spot," then put your dog back in the crate following the procedures mentioned above. It is extremely important that the dog cannot come out of the crate when barking or whining. Remember, ignore the bad & reward the good!

This is why having the dog close to you, near the bedroom, is good. Even though the first week can be rough, the puppy is still within ears, eyes and nose of you, which for them is comforting! All in all, the barking and whining has nothing to do with "hating the crate," but everything to do with a dog being a social animal and not knowing the household clock and schedule. Ultimately, it is your job to make the dog as comfortable as possible in a positive manner, while still teaching your new houseguest the rules and the difference between bedtime and awake time.

C. Dog has been in bed for several hours:

1. What if the dog quiets at first, but then starts crying later? This is not the dog trying to keep you up all night or train you. Something is wrong! Your dog might need to relieve himself, might need a drink, might be scared or any other possible reason. So get your bathrobe on, wait for five seconds of silence, get the dog out of the crate, on the leash, and take them outside. It is okay to talk soothingly to calm the dog, but do not scold or make this experience negative in any way. You would not do that with a child, and the same rules apply to your dog.

2. Remember, the only late night option is the potty spot. We do not want the dog learning bad habits, or teaching you any. So once Fido has a potty break, it is back to bed in the crate.

3. Do not fall into the trap of taking the dog back to bed with you! The bed is yours and reserved only as a reward! That's right, I do not have a problem with dogs sleeping in their owner's bed, but there are two non-negotiable rules

- The dog must be invited by you! After all, it is your bed, right?
- The dog must say please. Offer a sit, and patiently wait for the invitation.

So how long does your dog have to use the crate? Well, as long as it takes for Fido to learn to hold his bladder and bowels, as well as for him to respect the house rules (be trusted not to chew, mark, eat or dismantle the house in any way). Each dog is different, but my rule of thumb is 18 months to 2 years! Each dog is different, and the only way to test your dog's ability is to just do it. But in my opinion, anything less than 18 months is pretty much Russian Roulette! Eventually, adolescent behavior will rear its ugly head. I am a firm believer in errorless training, which means I will not give a dog the chance to make a mistake. So I err on the side of caution!

My dogs still sleep in crates today, only they rarely have the gates shut. But that only happened after several years of training and trust! A word of caution on the entire "freedom" testing: do not offer freedom to the entire house right off the bat. Remember, you should only work from small successes! First the bedroom, then include the hallway and so on.

And don't call your dog trainer complaining that your dog, left unsupervised, ate the chocolate cake off the counter in the kitchen! Just as with kids, before freedom always comes baby or kid-proofing, so they never learn bad habits! At this point, you are probably wondering if you bought a book on crate training or potty training. Well as a matter of fact, you have both! Just keep reading – I promise it only gets better!

Mistakes Equal Bad Habits

I look at potty training a little differently than most other trainers, by considering only one spot as the correct area to go to the bathroom. All others are wrong choices that just confuse the dog. Let's say your dog has had 12 accidents in the last week since you brought him home. You are pulling your hair out and things actually seem to be getting worse.

Well, I must apologize, but you are reaping the reward from the seeds you have sown! Yes, *you* are the one causing the problem. The problem starts because your dog does not speak English and you have not taken the time to learn "dog speak."

Before you get all indignant, let's stop for a minute to look at it from the dog's point of view. What is Fido getting out of his education? Fido now thinks there are 13 acceptable spots – that's 12 in your home and one outside – to go to the bathroom. The one outside is the one you, as an owner, desperately want the dog to use (the potty spot) but as of yet have not taught him to use; and the other twelve (all over your house) that he has been allowed to use (by you) that are incorrect. Hopefully this statement rings true as to the reason why potty training can be so difficult if not done right.

Unfortunately, most humans are not very consistent. We allow the dog to make mistakes and then blame Fido for not "getting it." This is where good management (mistake-free potty training) comes into play! You *cannot* mentally check out while there is a puppy or new dog in your house – remember, 60 days. You chose to bring this little ball of fur into your house and now you must invest the time to make sure every decision Fido makes is the right one! Not only does this mean showing the dog where the right spot is . . . which, by the way, I have not yet begun to discuss. But you must make sure accidents don't happen! If you remain vigilant that mistakes will not happen, the dog only learns what is right and potty training is a breeze!

However, we are all guilty of watching the boob tube, talking for hours to Great Aunt Matilda, feeding the kids and doing laundry. While all of this goes on, we ignore the dog at the critical moment when their urge strikes. Then the puddles and piles just magically appear, and before we know it, Fido is learning the wrong behavior, even if it's unintentional on our part!

The key is to use Fido's clean nature as a springboard, along with crate training, to eliminate mistakes and create only one choice of where to potty.

Science has determined that teaching people new behaviors takes approximately 21 times to create a habit. The same principle is true for dogs, but it probably takes closer to 40-50 repetitions to instill a reliable habit in a dog (thus the 60 day fanatical training). So your only chance for success becomes a fanatical first couple of months while you own Fido! You must make sure you take your dog out regularly, at least once an hour, to the appropriate potty spot, thus eliminating the option of making a mistake. Use the crate positively during those times when you mentally check out or when you're outside the home.

If practiced consistently, which is the real secret, Fido learns through his own choices and behaviors that there is only one place where he can do his business. Here is another one of those little secrets to aide in this process; tether the dog to you during the day while you are busy doing things that would normally take your attention away from Fido.

Here's a tip – and I know this sounds crazy, but it really works! Just slip a six-foot leash around your waist, attach the dog and get busy doing all the stuff you normally do during your busy day! You know, cleaning, laundry and cooking dinner. Now the dog stays with you, instead of slinking off to the back bedroom to leave his or her daily deposit in secrecy. Another added benefit to tethering is teaching good leash skills – but that is for another book!

By using the crate at night and when you cannot mentally keep an eye on the dog, you are guaranteeing that when you let them out of the crate, their bowels and bladder are full. And guess what? They have to go! Guaranteed success.

So what about when you go to work? And what about the dog's inconsistent schedule? Great! Let's break down some simple techniques to put you ahead of the curve and feel like you are back in control. Ready?

Let's get the one that will tick you off out of the way first, and then I will drop some really cool tips on you. *YOU bought, rescued, or were given and now have responsibility for this furry little monster,* so do not get upset when I tell you someone is going to have to check on the dog up to several times a day. I am sorry you have a job that makes checking on the dog hard or impossible. But if you expect potty training to go smoothly (mistake-free) then someone – yeah, that's you! – has to come home at lunch, come in late or even leave early to make sure no accidents happen in the crate.

Here's the good news: this process will only take approximately 60 days. So given that timeline, make plans, not excuses! Hey, if you are lucky, there are others in your household that can help. Spread the responsibility around. But remember, there is no excuse for a dog having an accident inside the crate other than an owner who left Fido there too long.

Don't forget other options: professional dog walkers, doggy daycares and even nice neighbors or outside family members who can help. But you, as the owner, must set this up or at least consider it prior to getting the dog.

Remember what my mom said about pre-work: don't call me, or any other trainer for that matter, to complain that Fido is nine months old and not potty trained because you "have no other choice" than to leave him crated for 12 hours a day. Really, dogs require work! People who buy dogs on a whim are the lifeblood of my training business, but unfortunately they are also the ones who rarely want to put the effort into training their dogs.

Some tough love: Only bring a dog into the house when you know you are going to have the time to spend with him, getting off on the right foot!

DO NOT BUY A DOG . . .
1. During the holidays
2. On an impulse (*Oh, how cute!*)
3. As a gift, especially a suprise gift
4. During a busy season at work

So when is it a good time to buy or get a dog? When you have a plan in hand prior to getting your dog, and you have some spare vacation time to do it, right?

Free feeding or leaving food and water out all the time is one of the biggest mistakes people make when potty training a dog of any age! It might sound strange, but let's face it, if you eat all day, guess what else you will have to do all day? No wonder it seems like Fido is going all the time.

What we need is a food and drink schedule that helps both you and Fido get on the same page and schedule. Let's say your veterinarian (who knows better than the back of the dog food bag) suggests Fido should eat three cups of food a day. (Yes, I have big dogs!) You should ideally feed his daily food ration in 2-3 portions, let's say morning, noon and early evening. If you work, and the dog is not a puppy, twice a day is okay: morning and early evening will do. Puppies should be fed at least three times a day (remember the entire pre-work conversation?) You might just have to get family, friends, dog walker or your kennel to help out with a puppy. But no matter who is doing the feeding, the dog should get about 30 minutes to eat, and then pick up whatever is left and back in the bag it goes until the next feeding time!

The reason for all this structure is to get your dog on a set schedule. Guess what else magically conforms to this schedule? You guessed it! Fido's pooping times! Now you have another weapon in the ever-growing arsenal of potty training! You will soon know the schedule like clockwork. For example, 37 minutes after Fido eats is **NOT** the time to get too involved watching reruns of Gilligan's Island, for fear of letting the dog choose his own toilet spot somewhere in your home.

Now comes your next logical question: what about water? While I do not recommend ever restricting water for a dog, I do recommend controlling when and how much water Fido can access at one sitting. With dogs that have a historical issue with piddle problems, a bowl of water will be present at meal times, because I know I will be taking Fido out soon to empty the bowels, so the bladder will just come along for the ride. However, as an option, I might put ice cubes in the water dish throughout the day. This is enough to hydrate our dog, but not enough to put pressure on the bladder and create the urge to void said bladder in spots all over the house.

Or, I might just periodically put out a small amount allowing the dog to drink, but not tank up. Let's use the example of kids again. Am I going to give my seven-year-old who sleeps very deeply, a Big Gulp right before bed? No! Maybe a small drink after brushing the teeth, but by no means am I going to tempt the Gods with lots of liquid – I do not like doing that much laundry!

The same principle applies to your dog. If the last feeding is at 6 pm and I go to bed at 10 pm, the water bowl should be picked up and put on the kitchen counter at 7 pm. That way, at 9:50 pm when I take Fido out for the last time, I know his bladder is empty. Yes, that darn pre-work again! If I am consistent in my food and water time frames, there is no reason (other than medical) for the dog not to be regular as well. That makes error-free training a whole lot easier.

I have even been known to ask clients to put a blank piece of paper up on the fridge and track the time and type of all pottying for a couple of weeks. Before they know it, they are seeing the magic pattern appear: 22 minutes after each feeding time, noticing the dog always seems to need to pee right before bed, and so on. I really think that inherently we know all this stuff, but life happens and we lose focus!

By forcing ourselves to be more consistent, we find ourselves winning more and losing less. Another plus is that time spent around Fido becomes less stressful. For the next step, all you have to do is pick a spot, more specifically a "potty spot," and just get your leash.

Choosing "The Potty Spot"

First things first: you, not the dog, gets to choose the potty spot. After all, aren't you going to be doing the poop scooping? In my opinion, I want one location to clean, not the entire yard.

One word of caution: pick your location well, because once the dog has been trained to a particular spot, changing it can be a real headache! Not to mention, most dogs will become accustomed to what ever type of ground they have been conditioned. So a dog that is used to concrete will always prefer concrete and might be stubborn on grass and visa-versa. Once the location is selected - pick a cue word. I use "Potty, Potty." I say the phrase twice; once to get the dog to the back door, and once to cue the action in the backyard. Some trainers will use separate words for each type of potty, and there is nothing wrong with that, so let's use Potty Pee and Potty Poop respectively for each type of deposit!

What about puppies? At early ages, puppies might be too young and unreliable to make it all the way to the back door by themselves. When they come out of the crate they are really going to have to GO! Don't expect to call them to the back door without a pit stop along the way! Remember the idea of mistake-free potty training. Start by carrying the puppy to the door while saying the "potty, potty" cue! As we progress, and the good habits for I will let them come to the back door on their own, but never right off the bat!

Any secreat weapons? Yes – it's the leash. A six foot leash works best for this. When the dog gets to the back door, whether by us carrying Fido or from those little legs, I put the dog on the leash and head for the potty spot! Yes, *you have to go with the dog!* For at least the first month, I expect you to walk the dog on that leash, to the potty spot and just stand there! Once there, plant roots like a tree and wait. The dog will be able to move around you, but Fido will not be allowed to wander all over the yard. This eliminates distractions!

You know that dog who spends hours (okay, it's actually minutes, but seems like hours when it's freezing, raining or snowing) just sniffing the ground. Look at it this way: in the beginning, the dog has yet to learn what you want! If you stick them in the backyard with little if any direction, and they are faced with every sound, sight, smell, touch and taste of the backyard to distract them, what do you think is going to happen? Meanwhile, you, the human, are getting ticked off because the dog is not focusing! In truth, the dog is paying attention, just not to what you want.

So by using the leash, you are teaching business first; sniffing, wandering and playing later. The leash simply gives you the ability to keep the dog's attention to a smaller portion of yard (not to mention the future permanent potty spot). Give the dog a reasonable amount of time to go, seven minutes tops. Don't forget to use the cue words occasionally (Potty, Potty), and especially when the golden moment arrives (i.e. Potty Pee and Potty Poop). When Fido is successful, celebrate! Say "Good Potty" (use the cue word, *not just "good dog"*) and give two or three treats.

Then, let Fido off the leash to play, allowing time to wander and sniff to that puppy heart's desire. This is the time to let your dog enjoy life – after business is done. The reward will become the chance to play and explore, if and only if the potty business occurs first. If nothing happens in that six to seven minutes and there is no potty progress, take the dog back inside and place Fido in the crate for 15-20 minutes and repeat the process. Yes, it will likely become a battle of wills, but it is a battle you and your carpet will appreciate! It might take an hour, but you must teach the dog that nothing fun happens until the potty business has occurred.

The dog also learns the backyard with the leash equals potty time (business first) and the backyard without the leash equals play time (the reward). Once this behavior has been learned, along with some other stuff still to come, the leash will not be necessary. Until then, use the leash and keep Fido focused on the task at hand!

So many people walk their dogs as a way to get them to "relieve" themselves. Nothing wrong with this, unless Fido begins teaching you (instead of you teaching your dog). The scenario goes something like this . . . You start off great, guns-a-blazing; walking the dog and everything is going great. The dog is peeing and pooping within five minutes and each time they do you say good dog, you might even give them a treat, but then you head back to house.

Here's the hiccup . . . within a week, it is taking 10 minutes, then 15 and the next thing you know you are a mile and a half from the house before Fido does his business. You are getting more and more frustrated and just don't understand what the heck is going on. Now don't shoot the messenger, but your dog is training you! Fido figured out a long time ago that he really enjoys walks, but his darn human always ends the walk the minute he poops and pees. So in his mind, Fido only has one choice to lengthen his walks . . . he must hold it for at least a half hour so that he gets his walk. Likewise, the human gets no pooping or peeing in the house.

Where-oh-where did you go wrong? Well, you focused on the wrong reward because you never learned to speak dog. All Fido really wanted was his walk! But those dumb humans were giving treats and praise instead of the one thing he really wanted: a walk.

So what now? Simple: from now on, commit to a 30 minute walk, but only after the business transaction is complete. Wait for Fido to poop and pee. Then and only then will Fido get his walk as the reward. In other words human training dog . . . not dog training human.

Let's take a look at another common potty training tool many people use, and one that I don't particularly like: the potty pad (or newspaper, for that matter.) Why would you give Fido a spot where you are okay with him peeing and pooping in the house?

Why? It's because you are convinced that you are too busy to spend the time on the process, and it is the only way that, with your busy life, you can accomplish the goal of having a potty trained dog. Let's look at this one logically instead.

If you're attempting a potty pad or newspaper, you're teaching Fido two things. You want to teach the dog to only go outside to relieve themselves, but you also offer an alternative . . . this is a confusing scenario for a dog! You're teaching the dog that going potty outside is okay, and going inside is okay: no direct command, no direct action.

For an extreme example, look to that $3,000 white persian rug in the dining room. Fido has learned that the house is an okay location for going potty; what's to stop your pup from choosing that $3K carpet over the $3.00 newspaper?

Now don't get me wrong, many people have used potty pads, and yes, it has worked. But it takes longer to get Fido 100% reliable. You have to train your pup to use the pads, then you have to go back and retrain them not to use the location. To me, the use of potty pads and newspaper is merely a crutch for those who (sorry!) are just too lazy to do it right the first time. In the end the decision is yours, but I promise if you follow the ideas contained here in my ramblings, you won't need those potty pads!

There is however, one reason for the use of a secondary *indoor* potty area – but it is not a potty pad or newspaper, it's a litter box. Over time, I have realized there are some folks who live on the 28th floor of an apartment building, and expecting Fido to make that elevator trip without an accident, well that's like asking a water balloon to hold Lake Erie. So in that case what do you do? Get a litter box and train the dog to use it! Many of you either currently have or had cats in the past, so you know it can be done. In this case, going in a litter box is a much better option than on your living room floor (or the elevator!)

To my knowledge at this time, there are two basic types; the "cat litter box" type and the "Astroturf" type. Both work and have positive and negative aspects. First, let's look at the cat litter box type available at most pet warehouse stores. Let me be very clear – I do not recommend cat litter.

Fido does not bury his poop, and the entire clumping thing will just freak him out.

Ask for dog litter. Yes, they do make it. It is essentially little nuggets that absorb moisture and smell. But just like the cat version, you will have to clean it and add new litter regularly or the smell will drive you right out of the apartment. Furthermore, just like a cat, a dog will find new locations for those deposits if that box is not clean.

The other drawback to this style of litter box is size: these boxes are only come in small and medium, which fits toy-sized dogs up to maybe a Cocker Spaniel size. Unfortunately, if you own a German Shephard or larger dog, I am not sure you want to be cleaning or refilling that box!

For those with larger dogs, the Astroturf style litter box might be a better choice. These are plastic boxes with a built-in tray that the turf sits on, so the urine passes through the turf into the lower section of the box and the pooping process is just as it would be outside. The drawbacks here? Smell. As you can imagine, the urine basin will fill and begin to smell after a couple of uses and the poop must be scooped regularly. If not, the smell will motivate you to keep it clean. But in the end, it is still better than Fido using the carpet!

Training Fido to use these options happens the same way that has been described so far, but ask yourself a simple question. Even with your lifestyle, even with your work schedule, even living on the top floor of that high-rise . . . don't you think, with the right planning and pre-work, you could do it without an indoor potty spot? I leave that up to you.

As a dog trainer, I am convinced that with the right techniques and effort, you could figure out how to avoid these options. But, as I said, that is a question for you and your family, the options are yours!

So if you're wondering how to know Fido has to go . . . read on!

How To Know They Gotta Go...

Just as with our kids, we don't give 100% freedom right off the bat to our dog. We start by teaching Fido to hold it and not to soil his crate. We then give him the appropriate place to go in the backyard. We use tethering and other management techniques so there's no chance for accidents! But let's face it, we don't plan to have our dogs tied to us or to watch them 24/7 for the next 8-12 years, so how do we start letting the dog know that there is no place in the house that is an appropriate place to potty? Start small. First teaching Fido not to soil in the kitchen, then include the living room and so on. Along with all of that, we must also find a way for the dog to tell us he has to go without us needing to look right at him when he decides he has the urge! This might sound like perfect sense, but in reality it is harder than it sounds. It's not difficult, but you have to be consistent!

I use baby gates and bells to finish up my potty training with dogs. Think of it as a graduate degree in potty training, a masters degree in Poop and Pee, if you will. I start in the kitchen with both a baby gate and bells. Why my kitchen? Easy access to the door to the backyard, where my potty spot is! The baby gate keeps the dog in a smaller area in which to learn, and the bells on the back door are so Fido can let me know he has to go potty when I am not looking at him or otherwise paying attention!

First, let me shed some light on one of the biggest mistakes humans make when it comes to the accidents our dogs have! Dogs are very polite animals and, given the choice, they would rather move away from their den or home to go to the bathroom. A person would never relieve themselves in the kitchen, and dogs think as we do. It would be quite rude to just take a dump so close to their family. So if Fido slinks off to the back bedroom to do his business, he doesn't know what he's doing is wrong. The fact of the matter is, you waited too long to take the dog out, or missed the signal telling you they had to go. So Fido just went as far away from their "home" as he could and did what he had to do! It is just the polite thing to do!

What about those dogs who pee or poop right by the back door? I love getting this scenario from clients. Most folks consider this the utmost insolence from the dog. But in reality, the dog made it to the bathroom door (door to the "potty spot") but you, the human, refused to open it! What did you really expect to happen? From a dog trainer's perspective, you have a dog that is 75-80% potty trained and you only need to find and train an appropriate way for the dog to ask **you** to open the door. Simply put, I use the baby gate to keep the dog in the particular room (starting small) and the bells as a way for the dog to tell us "get off your hiney and let me out before I'm forced to poop on the kitchen floor!"

But before we get to bell training, this brings us to an aspect of potty training that I have yet to cover: what signals do dogs naturally send us that we might miss or are just not paying attention to, in an effort to let us know they have to go? Well the list is huge, but let's look at some of the more common behaviors dogs give to let us know they have to go! Here are my top ten:

1. **Sniffing.** Many dogs will begin to sniff frantically for what you might mistake as no reason, but in reality the call of the wild has come and Fido is now actively looking for a spot. Take him outside!

2. **Circling.** Many times, right after the sniffing occurs, and sometimes independently from the sniffing, the dog will start almost spinning in circles (some fast and others slow.) Fido is telling you he has found the general spot and is now zeroing in on his target. Take him outside!

3. **Right after play.** Yes that's right, if you are playing with Fido, his bladder and bowels are going to get jostled around, and that alone can create the urge. So always take Fido out after any good play session!

4. **First thing after being let out of his or her bed or crate.** By being in the crate and not wanting to soil this area, you can bet Fido will have to go. Do not pass go, do not collect $200 – rather, take Fido outside immediately!

5. **Whining or barking.** This one is somewhat different than the usual attention seeking behavior we normally see from Fido. These vocalizations are just a little more urgent than normal. So when you find yourself giggling over Fido's funny little noises, you might just want to take the dog out before you start cussing!

6. **After feeding time.** This might be 20 minutes after meal time or it could be three hours, but if you have Fido on a set feeding schedule, you will know what time to take Fido out. (Do not free feed!) The pattern will take a couple of weeks to see, but believe me, if the food goes in at specified times, well the "you know" will come out regularly as well!

7. **Sit and stare.** This is for the Fido who is not a crier or whiner. These dogs, while silent, are wonderful at giving their owners what I like to call the "hairy eyeball," while sitting right in front of them. Fido silently staring at his owner in hopes Mom or Dad gets off their hiney and opens that back door before the carpet is soiled!

8. **Pawing at the floor.** Some dogs, like people, must have just the right lighting and comfortable toilet seat to get in the mood to make a deposit. Thus, they dig the area in and around the spot they have chosen to go; you know, to make it more comfortable. What this means for you inside the house is, if you see Fido digging or pawing the ground, it might be time to hit that good ole pause button and take a trip to the potty spot!

9. **Hysterically running between where you are sitting and the back door.** This behavior is very obvious and usually only missed during sporting events or really good movies that keep our attention too well...as Fido's eyes turn yellow, his legs are crossed and he's cussing his/her owner under his breath. Pay attention!

10. **Slinking away – the disappearing act.** The only choice left to our "best friend" when ignored to the point of exploding is to do what any self-respecting dog would do. He is going to excuse himself as far away from the family and the living area (or den) as possible. He will then go to the back bedroom to do his duty. (And we claim to be the more intelligent of the two species!) So if your dog has disappeared, you are probably too late, but go find him anyway. You might just have time to finally let him out.

So if you heed this list, you might just save your carpet and you might also be well on your way to becoming proficient in Dog as a Second Language (DASL).

Next comes teaching Fido how to, in a way, speak some English, if only to give him a way to let you know when he has to go. At least you will give him the knowledge of how to ring the doorbell when you are ignoring him in his moment of need! If this sounds like something you would like to try, read on!

The Doggy Doorbell

In the last chapter, I discussed how in addition to baby gates and management, I use bells on the back door. This is your dog's personal doorbell to ring when Fido needs to go outside. Welcome to bell training for your dog. With the right training, your dog will be going to the back door and telling you he has to go outside; thus eliminating those frustrating accidents by the door or in the back bedroom when you are busy watching the game on TV.

Bell training is as easy as reading a Psych 101 book! Seriously, have you ever heard of a guy named Pavlov? He was the father of Classical Conditioning and showed us that certain things that happen together can be related to each other, which creates associations. So when using bells, all you have to do is make the sound of the bells signal going outside. It really is that simple. You are already using your cue/command (Potty, Potty) twice - once to get the dog to the door and the second time when you're outside, to get the business done.

Now, the only difference will be that once your dog is at the door, you need to get them to paw and ring the bell before they go out the door. No, the dog is not actually going to just automatically ring the bell, and there is no Jedi mind trick to change this fact. You actually have to train the dog to ring the bell. Hey, I told you potty training would take at least a couple of months, so quit whining and keep reading!

You have successfully used the phrase "potty, potty" and you have Fido at the door! Now, take Fido's paw and ring the bell with it. Then go outside just like normal. You know, on leash, to the potty spot, wait and so on. As you add the bells to the picture, the dog begins to associate access to the backyard (and thus the potty spot) with the ringing of the bell. Don't give me that look, it does work. Did you train the dog that the doorbell at the front door meant people entering the house? Of course you didn't, they learned it on their own through repetition. That is exactly what is going to happen with the bells and the back door.

The big key to the bell training is to make sure you are consistent. Every time your dog goes outside, the bell must be rung so that the relationship between the bell and going outside is very clear. I still want you to use the leash at this point in training to make sure the dog goes to the potty spot.

The reason for this is to ensure the dog associates the bell with going to the bathroom, not just going out to check his or her P-Mail or to play. If you drop the use of the leash too soon, the dog might just train you to let him out 82 times a day to play and check things out in the back yard. However, if you associate the bell with the leash and going to the potty spot, Fido might just think twice before tempting fate and ringing the bell for any other reason other than pottying.

Think of it like this: "*Ooooh a squirrel! I think I will go ring the bell and get Mom to open the door and let the games begin!*" However, you know dogs make excellent people trainers and decide to react to Fido differently for ringing the bell! You put the leash on and take him directly to the potty spot. Now the dog is outside in the potty spot on the leash, not having to go to the bathroom and on top of that not gaining access to the squirrel!

After 6-7 minutes, take Fido inside to his crate, wait 15-20 minutes, then repeat this process 2-3 times until Fido performs! Next thing you know, Fido is on board with "ringing the bell means potty time, *not* play time!" You have successfully trained Fido, instead of him training you! Don't you feel smart?

So just how long should you spend taking the dog's paw and ringing the bell before you start to think the dog is daft, and that they will *never* ring the bell themselves? First off, be patient. Some dogs will pick up the process quickly: one of the dogs in our house learned it in just a couple of days! Others could take a week to learn and some could take even longer! As with all things concerning dogs, those who practice patience and allow the dog to learn will be rewarded. But those who force the issue will fail.

However, you can cheat with those who seem to take to the idea slower. Smear some peanut butter on the bottom bell and wait. As she attempts to get to the peanut butter, the bell will ring, and you take the dog outside! I usually save this technique for the dogs that are reluctant to ring or are skittish of the bells, to once again create positive associations! The trick here is the same as with any dog training: letting the dog figure things out on their own rather than us trying to force the dog to get it! As soon as the dog accidentally rings the bell, you, the smart dog owner, will say "potty, potty", put the leash on, open the door and take the dog outside to the potty spot. As time goes by, you decrease the amount of peanut butter until it no longer has to be used! If you don't like the idea of using food on the bells, use a vanilla scented doggy spritz; they will investigate that as well!

And when they inadvertently ring the bells, you will follow the steps to make the association between "potty, potty" and bells. Anything to draw attention to the bells and make them ring, even if by accident, will work. Your goal is to make that association between the bells and doing their business a solid one. Once it's established, it will be nearly fool-proof for the future. Something else to keep in mind: if you have multiple dogs in the same household, it will typically be easier to teach the bell ringing method since dogs learn by example. Our indoor cat has even learned to ring the bell to let us know the "indoor/outdoor" cat needs to be let in!

This is a good time to talk about placement of the bell and the type to use. The bell obviously needs to be hung at the dog's nose level and that will depend on the size of the dog. A Jack Russell will obviously need a different length than a Great Dane! Likewise, if you are dealing with a puppy, choose bells that can be shortened as Fido grows. If you have multiple dogs of different sizes, make sure the bells you use are break away style, but find ones that have bells at different heights. This allows the bells to be available for the smaller dog as well the larger one.

The idea of breakaway bells is critical. I have heard of and even seen dogs get caught up and hung by home-made bells. Be careful in your selection, and make sure they are made with snaps that release not only each of the length sections, but also the piece that attaches to the doorknob! Even though I don't like having to write this part, when it comes to our dogs, it's important that safety is always considered. No one wants to see something bad happen to our furry four-legged friends!

Is Punishment a Bad Thing?

Let's get right down to a big sticking point I have about potty training: punishment as a way to teach or correct. So, should we head down this slippery road? Well, most positive reinforcement trainers would emphatically say no. I, on the other hand, have no problem with punishment if it is defined the right way.

I don't want to focus too much on psycho-babble, but while getting my psych degree I learned that punishment, simply put, is anything that decreases the frequency of a behavior. So with that definition, if done right, there is a place for punishment (technically speaking) in potty training or dog training.

However, some people consider smacking the dog with a rolled up newspaper, rubbing a dog's nose in its own filth or spanking Fido as viable punishments when potty training. To me, these techniques are nothing more than harassment, if not abuse. Furthermore, they don't work. The real issue here has more to do with the definition of "punishment" and not whether or not we should punish. Let's face it, as trainers we must have a way to let dogs know that a mistake has occurred. But before you use any punishment there are some questions to ask yourself:

1. **Has the dog been trained or shown what behavior is correct?** If not, how on earth can you "punish" the incorrect behavior? Think about this example. I want you to sit down – so, my training method is simply to slap you every time you are standing, not giving you any other cues. How much learning is really going on?

2. **Is the punishment a part of learning?** Or is it simply turning you into something scary that the dog now has learned to avoid?

Let's look at some of the ways punishment can be used incorrectly, relating to potty training, as well as some tips on how to change it up for success!

First, let's look at the use of the "newspaper" as a weapon or "rubbing the dog's nose in it" techniques. These are definitely old standbys. Someone in the family probably used these methods. Many of you may have grandparents or parents that practiced these techniques and they appeared to work, so what's the problem? Even if they've been used before, and may have shown some success, it does not mean they are the right path to take! Hopefully after sharing the following examples, I will have at least converted a few more of you to attempt different options, or at least think about your actions before you "punish."

Have you ever met a dog that just flat refuses to come to his or her owner? What about the dog that always goes to the farthest room in the house to do their business? Okay, what about the dog that when they hear a change in your tone or get a dirty look from their owner, roll over on their back and pee on themselves or give the guilty little smirk or smile when the owner catches them doing something wrong? All of these behaviors can be directly caused by smacking a dog with a newspaper, hand or, God forbid, rubbing a dog's nose in its own pee or poop!

Once again we, the humans, are expecting dogs to speak English rather than us trying to understand the dog's signals. I don't care how hard you try; dogs will not and do not have the ability to learn English.

However humans, being at the top of the so-called evolutionary ladder, do have the ability to think abstractly and understand the actions and reactions of a dog. We are just a little lazy sometimes when it comes to using that massive grey organ located between our ears!

Let's look at it another way. Do babies, let's say at 18 months of age, have the language ability required to think and respond to verbal commands? What would you think of someone rubbing a dirty diaper in an infant's face for having an accident? As crazy as this example is, let's take it one step further. Do you think the infant in question would learn to avoid this adult or be fearful of this person or all people in general? As the child grows older, do you think the child might learn to hide their diapers or training pants from this adult? This last example puts into clear understanding the differences and similarities between dogs and people. As a human, I can give examples to help you see a situation from a dog's perspective; but trust me, dogs do not have the ability to see if from a human perspective. So who needs to be putting on that proverbial thinking cap going forward?

The dog that goes to the back bedroom or away from the family to do his business might well be doing it out of cleanliness as discussed earlier, but that same dog might also be doing it because his/her owner does a Jekyll and Hyde routine every time they see a turd on the carpet! A dog can and will learn it is safer to poop under the bed in the back bedroom because Mom turns into "Mommy Dearest" every time she finds the pile. It is a simple but effective self preservation technique to poop far away from the person who goes nuts whenever they find feces. Believe me, your dog is totally confused about what causes this tirade and has no way of connecting their action (poop) and yours (the meltdown), other than that their owner is totally nuts and cannot be trusted if a turd is anywhere in the vicinity!

Now let's look at the rubbing the nose in the waste scenario. This one is much the same, the only difference is from the dog's perspective. The dog feels it is not safe to relieve himself around this unstable human because they always flip out and rub my nose in my own crap. "I really love my human, but potty time cannot and will not happen while they are around." You are essentially teaching the dog that going to the bathroom is a bad thing especially if you (the owner) are around!

Dogs do not have the same ability to gauge or relate to the passage of time as we humans. When we physically abuse (different from punishment) our dogs, they see no correlation between the pile or puddle and the beating or rubbing in which they receive. Although you are trying to correct an accident, you wind up destroying the relationship between you and your dog! Otherwise, why has your dog learned to avoid you?

So just how do you punish or correct a dog that has already had an accident? **You don't!** If it has already happened, there is not a darn thing you can do about it, other than clean it up and admit you were not managing the situation well enough (remember tethering, crating, bells?) It was your fault, not theirs. Some of you will not like this statement, but the sooner you get over it, the faster you will get off the potty training roller coaster!

Now, if you just happen to catch your dog in the act, that is a slightly different story. Because the "potty" is happening right now, you have the perfect opportunity to attempt an intervention of sorts. My suggestion is first and foremost *not* to yell, clap, smack, squirt or do any of the other negative things you might have heard of to your dog. Instead, start by making my tone happy and excited then rapidly say "potty, potty" while running to the back door! My goal here is to hopefully startle the dog mid stream or turd and get them to follow me out the door to the right location and finish.

The focus here is not volume or venom; both of these only convince the dog that choosing to go to the bathroom around his/her owner is dangerous. Not to mention, it points out how seriously imbalanced said owner is around poop or pee. Instead, all you can do is try to make the best of a bad situation! In the end, you waited too long and really have no right to be cranky about the "accident."

Let me share a story about my son that will illustrate how "thinking you are doing the right thing" and actually doing the right thing are sometimes not the same. His kindergarten year was a challenge. He was the one talking out of turn, getting in trouble for having conversations that were not school-related during class and even outright arguing with the teacher at any time that suited him. According to my mother, I was the same way, but I personally don't remember any events like these in my past!

Needless to say, my ex-wife and I found ourselves in many a parent teacher conference discussing solutions and ideas. The teacher at one point suggested putting a piece of masking tape on his desk and using a tally mark each time he did something inappropriate and at the end of class each day, he and the teacher would sit down and discuss plans for making tomorrow better. We, as parents, would reinforce the plan each night and in no time we would have the problem under control.

The first couple of days there were about five marks per day. Then it grew to eight marks and by the end of the first month, he was tallying up 17 marks a day and began to tell us daily how much he hated school. This was, of course, not the result we wanted.

My wife and I set up another conference and I made the suggestion, based on my experience as a dog trainer, that we should modify the system to only tally those instances in which he did something correct. At the same time, my wife and I would start to coach him, giving him ideas on what could get him tally marks: good stuff, like helping hand out papers, always remembering to raise his hand before talking and never interrupting the teacher or other kids!

It was slow going the first week: he was only getting two or three marks per day. But then something happened. He got up to four marks one day, and we made a really big deal of it! Then five tally marks, and so on. What came next we did not expect. He started asking the teacher what he could do to get another mark! Before the end of that month, he was getting 15-16 marks for doing things right each day, and when we asked the teacher how the inappropriate behavior was going, she said it had pretty much disappeared.

In the end, it was not the punishment that worked; it was the focus on the behaviors we wanted. Sure, there were times the teacher would say, "Behavior like that isn't going to get you a mark," as a reminder, but we had to quit focusing on the mistakes to get progress on what we wanted. This is a pretty embarrassing story for a dog trainer to tell, but it shows how easy it is to get going down the wrong road while thinking you are headed in the right direction.

In the end, the best punishment is really redirection, not punitive action. If you focus on what your dog is doing right, behavior is going to improve! Focusing on the bad simply makes training of any kind unpleasant and painful for all involved! So even though the definition of punishment holds true, it is better and much easier to understand if we just look at it as redirecting the inappropriate behavior to a behavior we can reward, a behavior we want to continue.

What To Do If We Find Puddles and Piles

Even if we do everything right, we still have to resign ourselves to the fact that mistakes will happen. Behaviorally, how we handle them is critically important. But there is still one aspect of the mistake we have not looked at: the housekeeping side of the equation. It too is very important, and if not handled correctly, can also cause setbacks. So, how do we mop up the puddles and pick up the piles?

You must make sure that you clean all accidents quickly and thoroughly. If not, the dog may go back to the spot and, because of the scent, use the same spot again and again. Many experts estimate a dog's smelling capacity as 40 times greater than that of humans. While humans have a huge visual cortex and see life with their eyes, dogs are wired first through their noses and see the world through smells. So if the smell is not eliminated, many dogs will simply begin a routine that takes them back to their new proverbial bathroom – you know, the back corner of the dining room!

One of the most common mistakes people make is to use a cleaner with ammonia in it. But what is one of the main ingredients in urine? That's right, ammonia (well, at least byproducts that smell like ammonia). It's no wonder Fido keeps going back to that same spot in the back corner of the dining room: to his nose, you have been cleaning pee with pee!

There are several methods to clean up accidents. Some work, some don't and many fall somewhere in the middle. So let's look at some of the common products.

Enzyme-based liquid types: These sprays that basically have microscopic bugs in them that eat urine and feces, thus eliminating their scents! You can get enzyme cleaners that are targeted to specific types of stains or odors. Many pet care companies sell enzyme cleaners aimed at removing urine stains and odors from carpets and furniture. These enzyme cleaners sometimes use an oxidation method to remove the stain. When the enzyme cleaner soaks into the urine or feces stain, it helps catalyze a chemical reaction to remove the residue. This breakdown helps release the molecules that cause the stain and odor, removing it from carpet or other material.

While enzyme cleaners are able to chemically break down both stains and most odors, they do not provide sterilization or any anti-bacterial properties. In those cases where just the enzyme liquid cleaner is used, some people notice that once the liquid spray dries, the smell tends to creep back – and you run the risk of Fido returning to the scene of the crime. The problem is, you can never totally blot out all the wetness and so you leave some of the smell behind! However, the product is relatively inexpensive, and that's beneficial.

Dry powder cleaners: These are basically microscopic "sponges" filled with a special pet stain and odor remover solution. You simply work the powder deep down into your carpet. You let the worked-in powder stand 30 minutes or more while it "sponges up" pet stains and odors. Then, you simply vacuum the dry powder out of your carpet. It's that simple! Some also include a misting agent that allows the stain to loosen before adding the powder. The big difference with this process is not having to soak the area with cleaner but rather using a powder to absorb or wick the stain and odor away. Many will include deodorizers and repellents to use after the vacuum process, so they can be more expensive than just spray products.

Liquid-based "home-made" vinegar cleaners: White vinegar has been used for centuries as a household cleaning substance. Because it is acidic, it dissolves mineral salt deposits, a basic component of dog urine. Vinegar is harsh, with a pH level of 2.4 to 3.4. This level of acidity removes any lingering dog urine from surfaces. When using vinegar as a household cleanser, and especially on floors with a finish, it should be diluted with water by at least half. If you choose this method, be sure to test an inconspicuous spot first with the vinegar-and-water solution to see if it will damage the flooring!

Many pet owners swear by these types of cleaners for dog smells and stains, but in my experience it does not work any better than other options. In fact, I have seen some dogs go back to the spots after cleaning with vinegar! It works with some dogs and not others. Some dogs dislike the smell and don't go back to the spot for that reason, where others don't mind the smell and some are even attracted to it. Due to the inexpensive nature of vinegar, it's worth a try. But be willing to switch to something else if it does not work for your dog!

If vinegar alone does not work, baking soda can be used as an additive. Pour baking soda onto the area first, and then add the diluted vinegar-and-water mixture. This chemical reaction will cause the mixture to fizz. Baking soda has odor-absorbency properties and may help with particularly tough odors. This solution may damage hardwood floors, so once again, test on an inconspicuous spot first to ensure no damage will be done to the finish.

Household cleaners: This group is not in my potty training arsenal. For the most part, they simply mask odors and rarely remove stains. As mentioned earlier, using ammonia based cleaners to aid in potty training can cause dogs to go back to scene of the crime! Avoid these cleaners totally. Ammonia can be found in many cleaners, including window cleaners, floor polishing waxes, drain cleaners, toilet cleaners, bathroom cleaners, multi-surface cleaners, glass cleaners, oven cleaners and stainless-steel cleaners. Ammonia is a core component in numerous products, usually in a distilled form, so you'll want to check the ingredient label if you are trying to avoid using ammonia.

As a way to make sure that I get all accidents cleaned up, I always recommend the use of a black light flash light to periodically check your flooring area for accidents. Let's face it, many accidents happen without us even realizing it! It is always truly shocking when I bring out the black light after turning off the lights in a client's house! There are usually many more stains and spots than what they expect, but at least after using the light they know where to start cleaning. We might even find a spot the dog keeps going back to that the client did not even know was being used! It is a great way to make sure you know where and what accidents are happening! Black lights are not magic; they simply make certain things fluoresce, such as bodily fluids like blood, urine, feces and semen. Why do you think all those crime shows use them?

Now, what if you have tried everything and the smell is still present and Fido keeps using the same spot? This one is rarely discussed, **but consider your subfloor.** If you have not been fast enough or aware of spots where accidents have happened, there is a good chance that your subfloor, grout, sheet rock or other porous sections of the flooring or walls are holding both stains and smells. If all else has failed, you are going to have to either replace or block the smell. One easy way to accomplish this is through the use of enamel-based primers that can lock in the smell and stains of urine (as well as many other things!) This gives you a clean slate in which to start!

I always recommend using a bleach solution or other disinfectant on the spot first, allowing time to dry, and then rolling on the primer. I have found that water-based products, while smelling less offensive, do not block the stains or smells nearly as well as the enamel-based products. Sufficient ventilation is very important when using these products. The fumes are dangerous and can really get to you in a closed off environment. Proper use almost always gets you back to a point in which training is possible, though.

What about repellents? Most repellents are geared toward use in your garden, and use in the house is not really a good idea. There are other sprays that are offensive to dogs and are intended to keep a dog from wanting to go back to a particular area that you could use, though. The drawbacks here are, as with humans, not all dogs will find one particular smell offensive. And some dogs will actually search out and actively pee on these treated areas to cover the "nasty" smell with their own! Obviously you can see that would be counterproductive. The marketing for these types of products is aimed at the "magic bullet" population who has not yet come to the realization that the entire process is the only way to achieve real potty training success! Using these products along with other techniques may make potty training easier, but to expect that any product can train your dog is foolhardy at best. Without good management techniques and teaching good habits, no "potty training" products are going to work in the end.

One More Possibility

Lets say you have read the entire book and you think to yourself, *I swear I have done all this stuff and Fido is still pooping and peeing all over the house!* Well, you might be one of the rare dog owners that need one final piece of advice.

See your veterinarian! In some rare cases, potty training problems can have a medical explanation. Some medical causes that might cause potty training problems include:

1 Urinary tract infection
2. Kidney infection
3. Hormonal imbalance
4 Incorrectly done spay or nueter
5. Bladder stones
6. Cushing's disease
7. Neurological problems
8. Diabetes

Having your vet involved from day one is critical to any training protocol, especially if you suspect a medical concern. Since this is the last thing you are reading, my hope is that those of you who are not taking their dog to a vet regularly, will. Your vet is your partner in caring for your dog. Those who already take their dogs to a vet might consider making an appointment for a consult if nothing else seems to be working.

Conclusion

Upon getting to this chapter, I hope you are ready to conquer potty training along with your dog! Knowing now that you are the one who has to communicate with your dog, you are more prepared for the inevitable setbacks! So, how are you going to deal with them? This book focused on many pitfalls I have observed as a dog trainer and dog owner. It even included examples and tips to make things easier.

There is one big issue all humans deal with – not only with dogs, but with cats, birds, kids, husbands, wives and even the boss! It is frustration and anger. Ironically, whether you are dealing with dogs, wives or kids, anger always follows frustration. And let me tell you, there are frustrations galore when it comes to training a dog, potty training or otherwise. My hope in writing this book is to give you a road map for success for getting both you and Fido trained.

Unfortunately, there will come a time when things don't go right and that will lead to frustration. Frustration will lead to anger and then, well, we have all been known to do things that we regret in those situations! I know this to be true because I have been there. I don't pretend to be perfect, or have all the answers. I can tell you that I have lost my temper, yelled at my dogs, grabbed their collars, and yes, I have even lashed out and smacked them on the end of their nose! Am I proud of that? Not at all, but I think it needs to be said since we are all human.

We can learn from our mistakes. This alone is what separates us from other animals like our beloved Fido! I will not be the one who throws rocks at glass houses. Every day, week and year that goes by with the wonderful experience of being a dog trainer, I look back on the mistakes I made and strive to never make the same ones again. You will make mistakes. You might regret decisions you made in the past. The difference is this: the future is yours to choose. Don't make the same mistakes again. Learn from old mistakes – its even okay to make new mistakes! – and then learn from them as well. A wise man once told me that learning stops when you stop making mistakes, or when you continue to make the same ones over and over. Take a deep breath, think about what you want to happen . . . and then make it happen. Don't get caught up with all the stuff you don't want!

As far as potty training goes, my goal for you is to THINK and then revisit why you bought this book. Obviously something you were doing was not working, or you wouldn't have spent the money on this book. Be open to new ideas, be willing to stretch yourself and don't fall for the easy "quick" fix. Instead, you need to work hard, be consistent, and above all else, do what is right and reasonable in regards to your dog! Trying techniques or ideas that leave you wondering "Should I be doing this?" Then stop and think! Remember that we are the ones with all the grey matter and opposable thumbs! In the end, isn't that why they call it humanity?

I wish you all the best and know that in the end you will Keep it Simple Stupid, and Ignore the Bad & Reward the Good!

Mike

Afterword

Well you made it, folks, the end of the book! First, I want to say thanks for buying the book. And secondly, I really hope you got something here in these pages that will help you and your dog communicate better. The information in these pages has come from many years of helping folks with the come when called/recall problem. I promise if you put in the time, practice, and spend the time *with* your dog versus *against* your dog, really anything can be accomplished!

If you enjoyed the book, there's plenty more where this came from! We have several other books, as well as many videos on our YouTube channel. We have an active blog, Facebook and other social media outlets. You name it, we've done it – in an attempt to teach folks to speak Dog as a Second Language.

While writing these books has been a pleasure, my true passion is public speaking! I love spreading the word about positive, scientific-based dog training. Let's face it, there are many people out there who have no idea how easy it is to train a dog or how enjoyable it can be! So simply Google me, Mike Deathe, or visit our business page www.kissdogtraining.com [http://www.kissdogtraining.com] (and yes it does stand for Keep It Simple Stupid) if you or your group would like to have me come to give a presentation!

A final thought, and a request if you don't mind . . . as a small author, one of the greatest gifts you the reader can give me is a few minutes of your time and a review online of this book. This is information I am passionate about and I feel will help lots of people out there. I just need your help to get the word out! So with that being said, thank you for reading the book, thank you for buying the book and thank you for being a part of training your dog the Keep It Simple Stupid way!

Mike

www.ingramcontent.com/pod-product-compliance
Lightning Source LLC
Chambersburg PA
CBHW052043070526
44584CB00018B/2589